# L'ÎLE FANTASTIQUE
# FANTASTIC ISLAND

## Illustrated by Brenda Haw

Adapted from Puzzle Island, in the Usborne Young Puzzles series, by

## Kathy Gemmell

**Bilingual editor: Nicole Irving**
**Design adaptation by John Russell**

Language consultant: Lorraine Sharp

## Original story by Susannah Leigh

**Edited by Gaby Waters**
**Designed by Kim Blundell**

# Contents

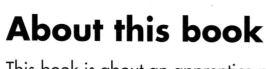

# About this book

This book is about an apprentice pirate called Max, his pet parrot, Percival, and their adventures on Fantastic Island. The story is in French and English. You can look up the word list on page 23 if you want to check what any French word means. This list also shows you how to say each French word.

Max

Le perroquet de Max, Percival
Max's parrot, Percival

Le bateau de Max
Max's boat

L'équipement pour l'aventure
Equipment for the adventure

## L'histoire  The story

Pour devenir un vrai pirate, Max doit trouver un badge à tête de mort.
To become a real pirate, Max must find a skull and crossbones badge.

Le badge est caché dans un coffre à trésor quelque part au coeur de l'île Fantastique.
The badge is hidden in a treasure chest somewhere at the heart of Fantastic Island.

Le badge à tête de mort
Skull and crossbones badge

Le coffre à trésor
Treasure chest

There is a puzzle on every double page. Solve each one and help Max and Percival on their way. All the French words you need to solve the puzzles are in the word keys (look out for this sign: 🗝). If you get stuck, the answers are on page 22.

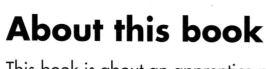 2

# Things to look for

During his journey to the treasure chest, Max must collect the nine pieces of pirate kit shown here. One piece of the kit is hidden on every double page. Can you spot them all?

*un chapeau de pirate*
a pirate hat

*une bouteille de jus fortifiant*
a bottle of fortifying juice

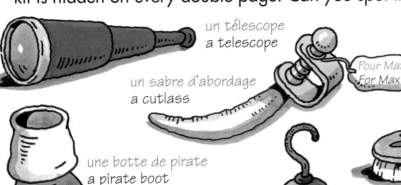

*un télescope*
a telescope

*un sabre d'abordage*
a cutlass

*Pour Max For Max*

*une boucle d'oreille en or*
a gold earring

*une botte de pirate*
a pirate boot

*un crochet*
a hook

*une brosse de perroquet*
a parrot's brush

*un sac de pièces d'or*
a bag of gold coins

## Horace the Horrible

Horace is a sneaky pirate desperate to beat Max to the treasure. See if you can spot him lurking on every double page.

Horace

## Pink elephants

Fantastic Island is home to the only remaining pink elephants in the world. There is at least one hiding on every double page. Can you find them all?

# How to sound French

Here are a few tips to help you say French sounds and letters in a French way:

à is said like the "a" in "India";
â sounds like the "a" in "part";
ai, ê and è sound like the "e" in "sell";
au and eau sound like the "o" in "rose";
e and eu sound like the "u" in "fur";
é is said like the "a" in "late";
i and y sound like the "i" in "machine";
oi sounds like the "wa" in "wagon";
ui sounds like the "wee" in "weep";

to say u, round your lips as if to say "oo", then try to say "ee";
ç sounds like the "s" in "sun";
ch sounds like the "sh" in "show";
you do not usually say the French h;
gn is said like the "nio" in "onion";
j sounds like the "s" in "measure";
n often sounds like the "n" in "aunt";
roll the French r at the back of your mouth, a little like gargling;
s, t, and r are usually silent at the end of a word.

# Le port  The port

L'aventure de Max commence un matin de bonne heure.
Max's adventure starts early one morning.

Il se met en route dans son petit bateau rouge.
He sets off in his little red boat.

Il dit au revoir à ses parents, à sa soeur et à sa grand-mère.
He says goodbye to his parents, his sister and his grandma.

Tout à coup, il pense à quelque chose d'inquiétant.
Suddenly, he thinks of something disturbing.

Il ne sait pas où se trouve l'île Fantastique.
He does not know where Fantastic Island is.

**Look at what people in the port are saying.
Can you spot what each of them can see?
Which person may be
able to help Max?**

## Key

| | |
|---|---|
| au revoir | goodbye |
| bon voyage | have a good journey |
| je vois | I see |
| un phare | a lighthouse |
| un cerf-volant | a kite |
| un vélo | a bicycle |
| une île | an island |
| une sirène | a mermaid |
| un phoque | a seal |
| un chat | a cat |
| un mouchoir | a handkerchief |
| une ancre | an anchor |
| ne ... rien | nothing |

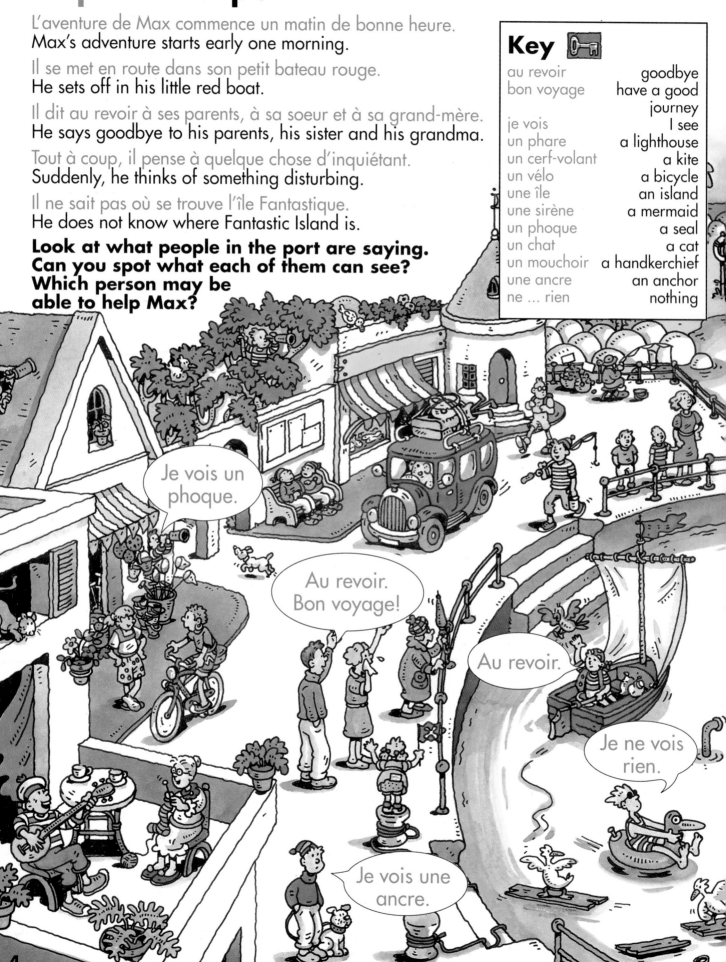

4

5

# Quelle île? Which island?

Max arrive bientôt dans un petit groupe d'îles.
Max soon arrives at a small group of islands.

Il regarde dans ses jumelles.
He looks through his binoculars.

Les îles se ressemblent toutes. "Laquelle est l'île Fantastique?" se demande-t-il. Tout à coup Percival crie: "Écoute!"
The islands all look the same. "Which one is Fantastic Island?" he wonders. Suddenly Percival squawks: "Listen!"

"J'entends des voix," dit Max, "et toutes parlent d'éléphants. Comme c'est bizarre!"
"I can hear voices," says Max, "and they're all talking about elephants. How strange!"

**Can you tell which island is which from what the animals are saying?**

Sur l'île Pomme, il y a un éléphant gris.

Sur l'île Cerise, il y a un éléphant violet et un éléphant jaune.

Sur l'île Banane, il n'y a pas d'éléphants.

6

# La chasse commence
# The hunt begins

Enfin arrivé sur la terre ferme! Max voit un panneau et plusieurs sentiers qui mènent dans une forêt.
Dry land at last! Max sees a sign and several paths leading into a forest.

Perplexe, il fait les deux choses écrites sur le panneau. Aussitôt, il entend des voix lui répondre.
Puzzled, he does the two things written on the sign. At once, he hears voices answering him.

“Ça y est!” s'exclame-t-il. “Je sais ce que je dois faire pour trouver le bon chemin.”
“That's it!” he exclaims. “I know what I have to do to find the right path.”

**Max must pass all the animals saying hello to reach the right path. Which way should he go?**

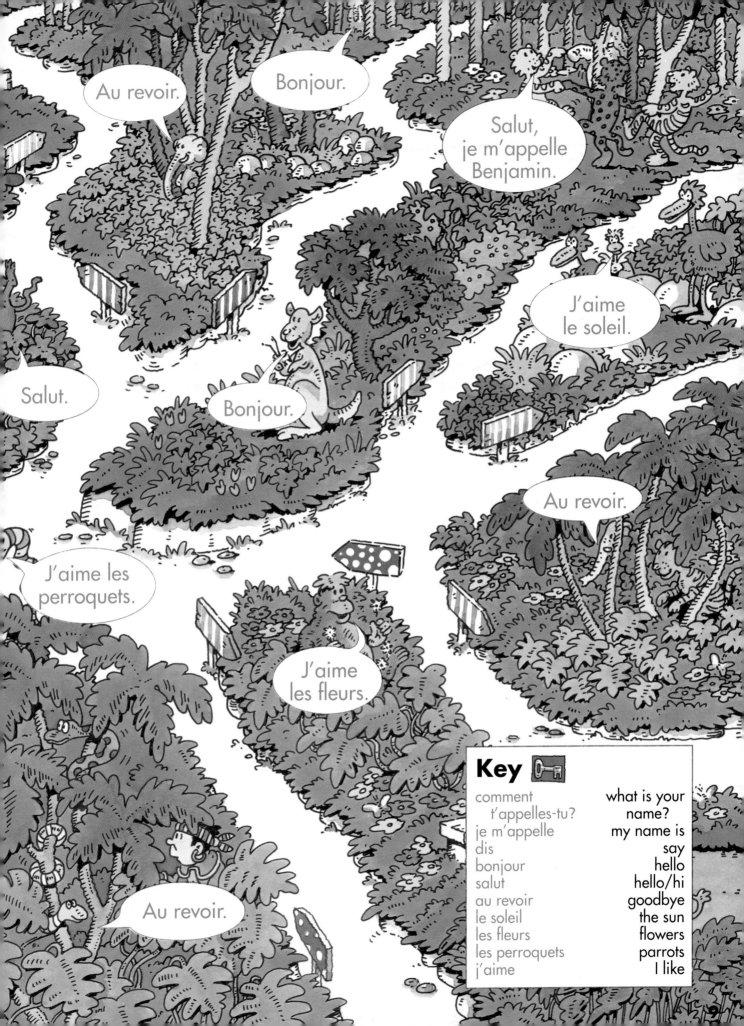

# Le lac   The lake

Max arrive bientôt à un lac couvert de feuilles géantes.
Max soon reaches a lake covered with giant leaves.

Il décide de le traverser en sautant de feuille en feuille.
He decides to cross it by jumping from leaf to leaf.

Max aperçoit un panneau au milieu du lac. Le panneau indique qu'il doit suivre les feuilles marquées de un à vingt.
Max spots a sign in the middle of the lake. The sign says he must follow the leaves marked one to twenty.

Max regarde désespéré. Toutes les feuilles paraissent numérotées. Sur lesquelles doit-il passer?
Max looks around in despair. All the leaves seem to be numbered. Which ones should he step on?

**Can you help Max count to twenty on the leaves to find the right way across the lake?**

## Key

| suis | follow |
|---|---|
| les numéros | the numbers |
| de | from |
| à | to |
| un | one |
| deux | two |
| trois | three |
| quatre | four |
| cinq | five |
| six | six |
| sept | seven |
| huit | eight |
| neuf | nine |
| dix | ten |
| onze | eleven |
| douze | twelve |
| treize | thirteen |
| quatorze | fourteen |
| quinze | fifteen |
| seize | sixteen |
| dix-sept | seventeen |
| dix-huit | eighteen |
| dix-neuf | nineteen |
| vingt | twenty |

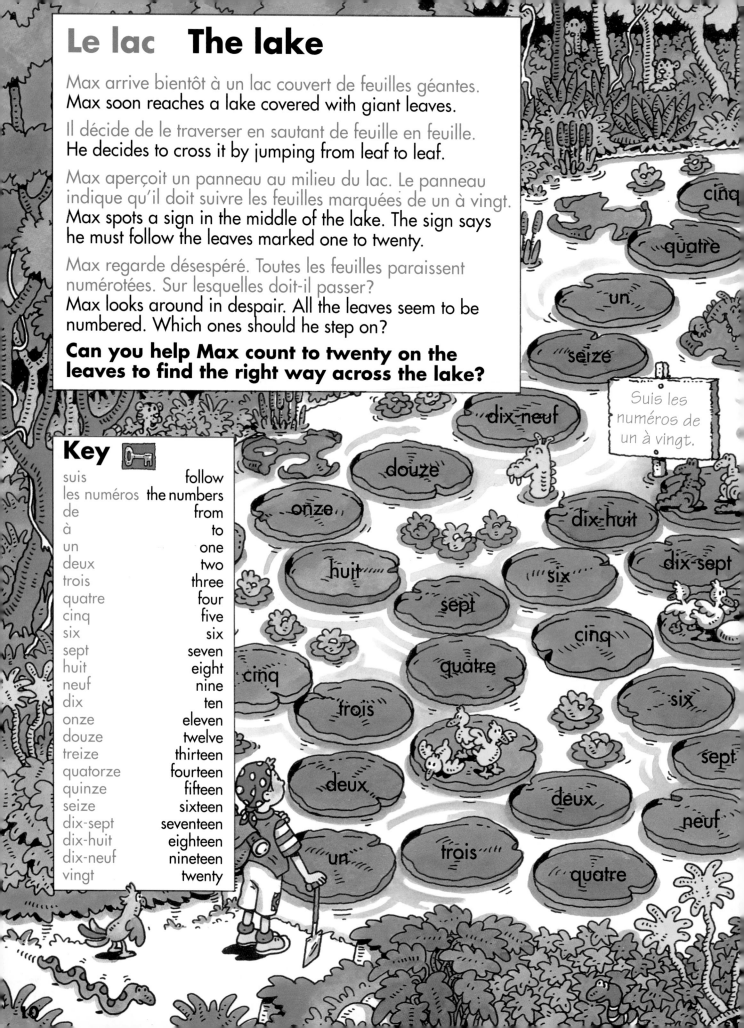

Suis les numéros de un à vingt.

cinq · quatre · un · seize · dix-neuf · douze · onze · dix-huit · huit · six · dix-sept · sept · cinq · quatre · cinq · trois · six · deux · sept · deux · neuf · un · trois · quatre

# Dans la forêt   In the forest

De l'autre côté du lac, Max voit quelque chose de très curieux.
On the other side of the lake, Max sees something very odd.

Un homme le regarde du haut d'une grande tour.
A man is looking at him from the top of a tall tower.

"Bonjour!" crie Max. "Savez-vous où se trouve le trésor?"
"Hello!" shouts Max. "Do you know where the treasure is?"

"Oui," répond l'homme, "je vais te le dire, mais d'abord, aide-moi."
"Yes," answers the man, "I'll tell you, but first, help me."

"Je cherche les six derniers animaux de mon livre des
Animaux Extraordinaires."
"I am looking for the last six animals in my book of
Amazing Animals."

**Can you spot all the animals the man is
looking for somewhere in the forest?**

Je cherche un lion,
un tigre, une girafe, un
singe, un serpent et
un chien.

Silence, s'il vous plaît.
Ne pas déranger.

**Key** 🔑

| | |
|---|---|
| je cherche | I am looking for |
| ne pas déranger | do not disturb |
| un lion | a lion |
| un tigre | a tiger |
| une girafe | a giraffe |
| un singe | a monkey |
| un serpent | a snake |
| un chien | a dog |
| et | and |
| (le) silence | silence |
| s'il vous plaît | please |

# Dans le verger  In the orchard

Le vieil homme dit à Max dans quel buisson il trouvera le prochain indice.
The old man tells Max in which bush he will find the next clue.

C'est une clé.
It is a key.

**Where does the label on the key tell Max to go?**

Quand Max entre dans le verger, il entend un bruit.
As Max enters the orchard, he hears a noise.

Un singe bleu marmonne quelque chose.
A blue monkey is muttering something.

**Should Max trust what the monkey says?**

Tout à coup, Horace jaillit de derrière un arbre.
Suddenly, Horace leaps out from behind a tree.

Il lance un filet sur la tête de Max.
He throws a net over Max's head.

**What is Horace going to do?**

Max se débarrasse du filet, mais Horace a déjà disparu.
Max shakes off the net, but Horace has already disappeared.

Puis il entend encore marmonner.
Then he hears more muttering.

**Where does the statue tell Max to go?**

Max se met en route pour le Château-Fantastique. Il arrive bientôt dans une clairière.
Max sets off for Fantastic Castle. He soon comes to a clearing.

Devant lui se dressent trois châteaux.
In front of him stand three castles.

**Can you use the statue's directions to answer Max's question for him?**

| Key 🔑 | |
|---|---|
| je vais | I am going |
| va | go |
| je mens | I lie |
| ne … jamais | never |
| toujours | always |
| quel est…? | which is…? |
| il n'est pas | it is not |
| trouver | to find |
| le trésor | the treasure |
| au | to the |
| (le) verger | orchard |
| (le) château | castle |
| rouge | red |
| jaune | yellow |
| avant | before |
| toi | you |

15

# Château-Fantastique
# Fantastic Castle

Max arrive devant le château bleu.
La grille est fermée à clé.
**Max arrives at the blue castle.
The gate is locked.**

"Cela doit être le Château-Fantastique,"
soupire Max. "Mais comment est-ce
que je vais entrer?"
**"This must be Fantastic Castle,"
sighs Max. "But how am I
going to get in?"**

Max pose son sac lourd.
"Voyons, je peux peut-être trouver
quelque chose d'utile dans mon sac."
**Max puts down his heavy bag. "Let's see,
perhaps I can find something useful in my bag."**

**Look at the contents of Max's bag. Can you find all the
things the weary adventurers need to keep them going?**

Le livre des pirates

L' île au trésor

Gâteaux pour perroquets

**Key** 🔑

| | | | |
|---|---|---|---|
| j'ai besoin d' | I need | un gâteau | a cake |
| je voudrais | I would like | (les) gâteaux | cakes |
| j'ai faim | I'm hungry | le livre | the book |
| j'ai soif | I'm thirsty | des pirates | of pirates |
| une clé | a key | l'île au trésor | treasure island |
| un chocolat | a chocolate | pour | for |
| (les) perroquets | parrots | et | and |

# Le repaire du pirate
# The pirate's den

La clé ouvre facilement la grille. Max et les perroquets fouillent le château.

The key opens the gate easily. Max and the parrots search the castle.

Quand ils entrent dans la dernière pièce, Max s'exclame, "C'est le repaire d'un pirate. Nous sommes presque arrivés!"

As they enter the last room, Max exclaims, "This is a pirate's den. We're nearly there!"

"Mais quelle est la bonne porte pour trouver le trésor?"

"But which is the right door for the treasure?"

Les souris du pirate sont très aimables. Malheureusement pour Max, elles sont aussi très myopes.

The pirate's mice are very friendly. Unluckily for Max, they are also very near-sighted.

**The correct door is the only one which fits one of the mice's descriptions. Which door is it?**

**19**

# Le trésor  The treasure

Max ouvre la porte. Il voit un sentier et le suit jusqu'à une immense cascade.

Max opens the door. He sees a path and follows it to a huge waterfall.

"Regarde!" il crie à Percival. "Une croix sur le sol. Creusons ici!"

"Look!" he yells to Percival. "A cross on the ground. Let's dig here!"

Pendant qu'il creuse, Max se rend compte qu'on l'observe.

As he digs, Max realizes that he is being watched.

**What is everyone telling Max to do?**

## Key 🔑

| | |
|---|---|
| vite | quick |
| dépêche-toi | hurry up |
| je cherche | I am looking for |
| une montre | a watch |
| une moto | a motorcycle |
| une voiture | a car |
| un ballon | a ball |
| une perruque | a wig |
| un badge | a badge |
| (la) tête de mort | skull and crossbones |
| (les) patins à roulettes | rollerskates |
| des | some |

Tout à coup, la pelle de Max heurte quelque chose de dur. Le coffre à trésor!
Suddenly, Max's spade hits something hard. The treasure chest!

Tout le monde se précipite pour aider Max à sortir le coffre.
Everyone hurries to help Max lift out the chest.

Max saute de joie. Enfin il est un vrai pirate, et en plus il a beaucoup de nouveaux amis.
Max leaps for joy. At last he is a real pirate and he has lots of new friends as well.

**Can you spot all the things that Max and his new friends are looking for?**

# Answers

## Pages 4-5

The objects that people can see are circled. This lookout may be able to help Max.

## Pages 6-7

Here you can see which island is which.

L'île Banane

L'île Fantastique

L'île Framboise

L'île Pomme

L'île Cerise

L'île Fraise

## Pages 8-9

The path Max should take is shown in black.

## Pages 10-11

The leaves Max should step on are shown by the black line.

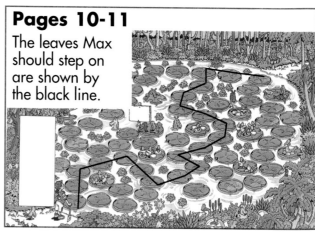

## Pages 12-13

The animals the old man is looking for are circled.

## Pages 14-15

The label tells Max to go to the orchard. He should not trust what the monkey says because the monkey always lies. Horace says he is going to find the treasure before Max. The statue tells Max to go to Fantastic Castle. Fantastic Castle is the blue castle.

## Pages 16-17

The things Max and the parrots need are circled.

## Pages 18-19

This is the correct door.

This mouse gives the right description.

## Pages 20-21

Everyone is telling Max to hurry up. The things that Max and his new friends are looking for are circled.

## Did you spot everything?

| Pages | Pink elephants | Equipment |
| --- | --- | --- |
| 4-5 | two | pirate boot |
| 6-7 | one | fortifying juice |
| 8-9 | six | telescope |
| 10-11 | two | gold earring |
| 12-13 | three | hook |
| 14-15 | two | gold coins |
| 16-17 | three | parrot's brush |
| 18-19 | two | cutlass |
| 20-21 | three | pirate hat |

Did you remember to find Horace? Look back and spot him on every double page.

# Word list and pronunciation guide

Here is a list of the French words used in this book. All the nouns (naming words) have le, la, l' or les before them. These all mean "the". In French, all nouns are either masculine or feminine. You use le with masculine nouns and la with feminine nouns. If a noun is plural (more than one), you use les. If it starts with a, e, i, o or u, and usually h, you use l'. Both l' and les nouns have [m] or [f] after them to show if they are masculine or feminine.

Some French describing words (adjectives) change when describing feminine nouns. Here, the masculine word is written first, then the feminine word. When an adjective describes a plural noun, it usually has an "s" on the end, as in: les fleurs rouges (red flowers).

Each French word in this list has its pronunciation shown after it (in letters like this). Read these letters as if they were English words. You will sometimes see (n) or (m), which you should say through your nose, as if you had a cold. You can read more about how to say French words on page 3.

| French | Pronunciation | English |
|---|---|---|
| à | ah | to OR at |
| ...a disparu | ah deesparew | has disappeared |
| aide-moi | ed mwa | help me |
| aider | edday | to help |
| aimable | emabl | friendly |
| les amis [m] | laiz amee | friends |
| l'ancre [f] | lonkr | anchor |
| les animaux [m] | laiz aneemo | animals |
| ...aperçoit | apairswa | ...spots |
| l'arbre [m] | larbr | tree |
| ...arrive | areev | ...arrives |
| arrivé, arrivée | areevai | arrived |
| au milieu | oh meel yuh | in the middle |
| au revoir | oh ruh vwar | goodbye |
| aussi | ohsee | also |
| aussitôt | ohsee toh | at once |
| autre | ohtr | other |
| avant | avo(n) | before |
| l'aventure [f] | lavo(n)tewr | adventure |
| le badge | luh badj | badge |
| le ballon | luh balo(n) | ball |
| la banane | la banan | banana |
| le bateau | luh batoh | boat |
| beaucoup | bokoo | a lot |
| bientôt | bee a(n)toh | soon |
| bizarre | bee zar | strange |
| blanc, blanche | blo(n), blo(n)sh | white |
| bleu, bleue | bluh | blue |
| bon, bonne | bo(n), bonn | good |
| bonjour | bo(n)joor | hello |
| bon voyage | bo(n) vwa yaj | have a good trip |
| la botte | la bot | boot |
| la boucle d'oreille | la bookl doraiy | earring |
| la bouteille | la bootaiy | bottle |
| la brosse | la bross | brush |
| le bruit | luh brwee | noise |
| le buisson | luh bweesso(n) | bush |
| caché, cachée | kashai | hidden |
| la cascade | la kaskad | waterfall |
| ça y est | sah ee ai | that's it |
| le cerf-volant | luh sair volo(n) | kite |
| la cerise | la suh reez | cherry |
| c'est | sai | it is |
| le chapeau | luh shapoh | hat |
| la chasse | la shass | hunt |
| le chat | luh sha | cat |
| le/les château(x) | luh/lay shatoh | castle(s) |
| le chemin | luh shuh ma(n) | way OR path |
| le chien | luh shee a(n) | dog |
| le chocolat | luh sho ko lah | chocolate |
| les choses [f] | lay shoz | things |
| cinq | sank | five |
| la clairière | la klair yair | clearing |
| la clé | la klay | key |
| le coeur | luh kur | heart |
| le coffre à trésor | luh koffr ah traizor | treasure chest |
| comme | kom | as OR how |
| ...commence | kommo(n)ss | ...starts |
| comment | kommo(n) | how |
| comment t'appelles-tu? | kommo(n) tapell tew | what is your name? |
| le côté | luh koh tai | side |
| couvert, couverte | koovair, koovairt | covered |
| creusons | kruh zo(n) | let's dig |
| ...crie | ...kree | ...shouts |
| le crochet | luh kroh shay | hook |
| la croix | la krwah | cross |
| curieux, curieuse | kewr yuh, kewr yuz | curious OR odd |
| d'abord | dabor | first |
| dans | do(n) | in |
| de, d' | duh | of OR from |
| de bonne heure | duh bonn uhr | early |
| déjà | dayja | already |
| dépêche-toi | daypesh twah | hurry up |
| dernier, dernière | dern yay, dern yair | last |
| derrière | derryair | behind |
| désespéré(e) | dayzespairai | in despair |
| deux | duh | two |
| devant | duhvo(n) | in front of |
| devenir | duh vuhneer | to become |
| dire | deer | to say OR to tell |
| dis | dee | say |
| ...dit | dee | ...says OR tells |
| dix | deess | ten |
| dix-huit | deez weet | eighteen |
| dix-neuf | deez nuhf | nineteen |
| dix-sept | deessett | seventeen |
| ...dois/...doit | dwah | ...must |
| doit-il...? | dwah teel | should he...? |
| douze | dooz | twelve |
| dur, dure | dewr | hard |

**23**

| French | Pronunciation | English |
|---|---|---|
| écoute | aykoot | listen |
| écrit, écrite | aykree, aykreet | written |
| l'éléphant [m] | laylayfo(n) | elephant |
| encore | o(n)kor | more OR again |
| enfin | o(n)fa(n) | at last |
| en plus | o(n) plewss | as well |
| en sautant | o(n) sohto(n) | by jumping |
| ...entre (dans) | o(n)tr do(n) | ...enters OR goes in |
| entrer (dans) | o(n)tray do(n) | to enter |
| l'équipement [m] | laykeep mo(n) | equipment |
| ...est | ai | ...is |
| est-ce que...? | ess kuh | is it...? |
| et | ay | and |
| être | aitr | to be |
| extraordinaire | extror dee nair | amazing |
| facilement | fasseelmo(n) | easily |
| faire | fair | to do OR to make |
| fantastique | fontasteek | fantastic |
| fermé/fermée à clé | fairmai ah klay | locked |
| la feuille | la fuh ee | leaf |
| le filet | luh feelay | net |
| les fleurs [f] | lay flur | flowers |
| la forêt | la forai | forest |
| fortifiant, fortifiante | fortee feeo(n), fortee feeo(n)t | fortifying |
| ...fouillent | foo yuh | ...search |
| la fraise | la fraiz | strawberry |
| la framboise | la frombwaz | raspberry |
| le/les gâteau(x) | luh/lay gatoh | cake(s) |
| géant, géante | jay o(n), jay o(n)t | giant |
| la girafe | la jeeraff | giraffe |
| grand, grande | gro(n), gro(n)d | big |
| la grand-mère | la gro(n) mair | grandma |
| la grille | la greey | gate |
| gris, grise | gree, greez | grey |
| le groupe | luh groop | group |
| le haut | luh oh | top |
| ...heurte | uhrt | ...hits |
| l'histoire [f] | leesstwar | story |
| l'homme [m] | lom | man |
| huit | weet | eight |
| ici | eessee | here |
| il | eel | he OR it |
| il creuse | eel kruhz | he digs |
| il décide de | eel dayseed duh | he decides |
| il entend | eel o(n)to(n) | he hears |
| il fait | eel fai | he does |
| l'île [f] | leel | island |
| il lance | eel lo(n)ss | he throws |
| il ne sait pas | eel nuh sai pah | he does not know |
| il n'est pas | eel nai pah | he/it is not |
| il n'y a pas | eel nyah pah | there are no |
| il pense | eel po(n)ss | he thinks |
| ils entrent | eel zo(n)tr | they enter |
| il trouvera | eel troovuh rah | he will find |
| il y a | eel ee a | there is OR there are |
| immense | eemo(n)ss | huge |
| l'indice [m] | la(n)deess | clue |
| ...indique | a(n)deek | ...shows OR says |

| French | Pronunciation | English |
|---|---|---|
| inquiétant, inquiétante | a(n)kee aito(n), a(n)kee aito(n)t | disturbing OR worrying |
| j'ai besoin de/d' | jai buhzwa(n) duh | I need |
| j'ai faim | jai fa(m) | I am hungry |
| ...jaillit | ja yee | ...leaps out |
| j'aime | jaim | I like |
| j'ai soif | jai swaff | I am thirsty |
| jaune | jone | yellow |
| je cherche | juh shersh | I am looking for |
| j'entends | jo(n)to(n) | I hear |
| je m'appelle | juh mapell | my name is |
| je mens | juh mo(n) | I lie |
| je peux | juh puh | I can |
| je sais | juh sai | I know |
| je vais | juh vai | I am going |
| je vois | juh vwah | I see |
| je voudrais | juh voodrai | I would like |
| la joie | la jwah | joy |
| les jumelles [f] | lay jewmell | binoculars |
| le jus | luh jew | juice |
| jusqu'à | jewss kah | until |
| le lac | luh lak | lake |
| le lion | luh leeo(n) | lion |
| le livre | luh leevr | book |
| lourd, lourde | loor, loord | heavy |
| lui | lwee | to him OR to her |
| mais | mai | but |
| malheureusement | mal uhr uhz mo(n) | unluckily |
| ...marmonne | marmonn | ...mutters |
| marmonner | marmonnay | to mutter |
| marqué, marquée | markai | marked |
| le matin | luh mata(n) | morning |
| ...mènent | menn | ...lead |
| la montre | la mo(n)tr | watch |
| mon, ma, mes | mo(n), ma, may | my |
| la moto | la mohtoh | motorcycle |
| le mouchoir | luh mooshwar | handkerchief |
| myope | mee yop | near-sighted |
| ne ... jamais | nuh jamai | never |
| ne pas déranger | nuh pa day ro(n)jay | do not disturb |
| ne ... rien | nuh ree a(n) | nothing |
| neuf | nuhf | nine |
| noir, noire | nwar | black |
| nous sommes | noo som | we are |
| nouveau, nouvelle | noo voh, noo vell | new |
| les numéros [m] | lay newmay roh | numbers |
| numéroté(e) | newmay rohtai | numbered |
| ...observe | obsairv | ...is watching |
| on | o(n) | (some)one |
| onze | o(n)z | eleven |
| l'or [m] | lor | gold |
| orange | oro(n)j | orange |
| où | oo | where |
| oui | oo ee | yes |
| ...ouvre | oovr | ...opens |
| le panneau | luh pannoh | sign |
| ...paraissent | paraiss | ...seems |
| les parents [m] | lay paro(n) | parents |
| ...parlent | parl | ...speak OR talk |

| | | | | | |
|---|---|---|---|---|---|
| passer | *passay* | to pass | ...se ressemblent | *suh ruhsso(m)bl* | ...look the same |
| les patins [m] à roulettes | *lay pata(n) ah roolett* | roller skates | le serpent | *luh sairpo(n)* | snake |
| la pelle | *la pell* | spade | ...se trouve | *suh troov* | ...is |
| pendant | *po(n)do(n)* | as OR during | ...s'exclame | *saix klam* | ...exclaims |
| perplexe | *pairplex* | puzzled | s'exclame-t-il | *saix klam teel* | he exclaims |
| le perroquet | *luh perrokay* | parrot | le silence | *luh seelo(n)ss* | silence |
| la perruque | *la perrewk* | wig | s'il vous plaît | *seel voo plai* | please |
| petit, petite | *puhtee, puhteet* | small | le singe | *luh sa(n)j* | monkey |
| peut-être | *puh tetr* | perhaps | la sirène | *la see renn* | mermaid |
| le phare | *luh far* | lighthouse | six | *seess* | six |
| le phoque | *luh fok* | seal | la soeur | *la suhr* | sister |
| la pièce | *la pee ess* | room OR coin | le sol | *luh sol* | ground |
| le pirate | *luh pee rat* | pirate | le soleil [m] | *luh soh laiy* | sun |
| plusieurs | *plewz yuhr* | several | son, sa, ses | *so(n), sa, say* | his OR her |
| la pomme | *la pom* | apple | ...sont | *so(n)* | ...are |
| le port | *luh por* | port | sortir... | *sorteer* | to lift out OR to take out |
| la porte | *la port* | door | les souris [f] | *lay sooree* | mice |
| ...pose | *poz* | ...puts | suis | *swee* | follow |
| pour | *poor* | for OR in order to | ...suit | *swee* | ...follows |
| prends | *pro(n)* | take | suivre | *sweevr* | to follow |
| presque | *presskuh* | nearly | sur | *sewr* | on |
| prochain, prochaine | *prosha(n), proshenn* | next | le télescope | *luh taylayskop* | telescope |
| puis | *pwee* | then | la terre ferme | *la tair fairm* | dry land |
| quand | *ko(n)* | when OR as | la tête | *la tet* | head |
| quatorze | *katorz* | fourteen | la tête de mort | *la tet duh mohr* | skull and crossbones |
| quatre | *katr* | four | le tigre | *luh teegr* | tiger |
| que, qu' | *kuh, k* | that | toi | *twah* | you |
| quel, quelle | *kel* | which | toujours | *toojoor* | always |
| quelque chose | *kelkuh shoz* | something | la tour | *la toor* | tower |
| quelque part | *kelkuh par* | somewhere | tous, toutes | *tooss, toot* | all OR they all |
| qui | *kee* | who | tout à coup | *toot ah koo* | suddenly |
| quinze | *ka(n)z* | fifteen | tout le monde | *too luh mo(n)d* | everyone |
| ...regarde | *ruh gard* | look | traverser | *tra vairsay* | to cross |
| le repaire | *luh ruhpair* | den | treize | *trez* | thirteen |
| répond | *raypo(n)* | answers | très | *trai* | very |
| répondre | *raypo(n)dr* | to answer | le trésor | *luh traizor* | treasure |
| rose | *roz* | pink | trois | *trwah* | three |
| rouge | *rooj* | red | trouver | *troovay* | to find |
| le sabre d'abordage | *luh sabr dabordaj* | cutlass | un, une | *a(n), ewn* | one OR a |
| le sac | *luh sak* | bag | utile | *ewteel* | useful |
| salut | *salew* | hello OR hi | va | *vah* | go |
| ...saute | *soht* | ...jumps | le vélo | *luh vaylo* | bicycle |
| savez-vous...? | *savay voo* | do you know...? | le verger | *luh vairjay* | orchard |
| ...se débarrasse | *suh day barass* | ...shakes off | vert, verte | *vair, vairt* | green |
| se demande-t-il | *suh duhmo(n)d teel* | he wonders | vieux, vieil, vieille | *vee yuh, vee aiy* | old |
| ...se dressent | *suh dress* | ...stand | vingt | *va(n)* | twenty |
| seize | *sez* | sixteen | violet, violette | *vee olay, vee olet* | purple |
| ...se met en route | *suh mett o(n) root* | ...sets off | vite | *veet* | quick |
| le sentier | *luh so(n)tee ay* | path | ...voit | *vwah* | ...sees |
| ...se précipite | *suh prayssee peet* | ...hurries | la voiture | *la vwah tewr* | car |
| sept | *sett* | seven | les voix [f] | *lay vwah* | voices |
| ...se rend compte | *suh ro(n) ko(m)t* | ...realizes | voyons | *vwayo(n)* | let's see |
| | | | vrai, vraie | *vrai* | real OR true |

This bilingual edition first published in 1995 by Usborne Publishing Ltd., Usborne House, 83-85 Saffron Hill, London EC1N 8RT.
Based on a previous title first published in 1990. First published in America, March 1996.